T0199186

THE NEW EARTH PRESCRIPTION:

MEDITATIONS TO ACHIEVE A SUSTAINABLE VICTORIOUS LIFE

Elizabeth Salamanca-Brosig, PharmD

A Devotional on Health and Wellness for the Entire Family.

*Scriptures taken from the Holy Bible, New International Version®, NIV®. Copyright© 1973, 1978, 1984, 2011 by Biblica, Inc.™ Used by permission of Zondervan. All rights reserved worldwide. WWW.ZONDERVAN.COM"
"The "NIV" and "New International Version" are trademarks registered in the United States Patent and Trademark Offices by Biblica, Inc.™

WestBow Press books may be ordered through booksellers or by contacting:

WestBow Press
A Division of Thomas Nelson & Zondervan
1663 Liberty Drive
Bloomington, IN 47403
www.westbowpress.com
1 (866) 928-1240

Because of the dynamic nature of the Internet, any web addresses or links contained in this book may have changed since publication and may no longer be valid. The views expressed in this work are solely those of the author and do not necessarily reflect the views of the publisher, and the publisher hereby disclaims any responsibility for them.

Any people depicted in stock imagery provided by Getty Images are models, and such images are being used for illustrative purposes only.
Certain stock imagery © Getty Images.

ISBN: 978-1-9736-5432-2 (sc)
ISBN: 978-1-9736-5433-9 (e)

Print information available on the last page.

WestBow Press rev. date: 03/12/2019

WESTBOW
PRESS®
A DIVISION OF THOMAS NELSON
& ZONDERVAN

This book belongs to:

_____

This book is dedicated to my children Kylie, Kai and family.

See, I will create new heavens and a new earth. The former things will not be remembered, nor will they come to mind. But be glad and rejoice forever in what I will create, for I will create Jerusalem to be a delight and its people a joy. I will rejoice over Jerusalem and take delight in my people; the sound of weeping and of crying will be heard in it no more (Isaiah 65:17-19).

Keep this book (The Holy Bible) of the law always on your lips; meditate on it day and night, so that you may be careful to do everything written in it. Then you will be prosperous and successful. Have I have not commanded you? Be strong and courageous. Do not be afraid: do not be discouraged, for the Lord your God will be with you wherever you go (Joshua 1:8-9).

For the Word of God is alive and active. Sharper than any double-edged sword, it penetrates even to the dividing soul and spirit, joints and marrow; it judges the thoughts and attitudes of the heart. Nothing in all creation is hidden from God's sight. Everything is uncovered and laid bare before the eyes of him to whom we must give account (Hebrews 4:12-13).

Surely God is my help; the Lord is the one who sustains me (Psalm 54:4).

Where there is no revelation, people cast off restraint; but blessed is the one who heeds wisdom's instruction (Proverbs 29:18).

The Lord's Prayer

Our Father in Heaven, hallowed be your name, your kingdom come, your will be done, on earth as it is in heaven. Give us today our daily bread. And forgive us our debts, as we also have forgiven our debtors. And lead us not into temptation, but deliver us from the evil one (Matthew 6:9-13).

Contents

M2 = Be Armed in Truth.
YOUr Dreams MATTER.
Like an athlete trains, so must the student of life.
Train the mind, body and spirit, so you may achieve anything.
Life is about sharing your dreams/purpose (gifts/passions/
talents) with the world and helping others find their way.

This book is designed to introduce God's healing prescription, life-giving words of truth from the Holy Bible (2 Timothy 3:16), His gift to all of mankind. Two thousand years ago, God gave the world His one and only Son named, Jesus (John 3:16-21), to be a living witness testimony to all of mankind of God's existence (John 1:18).

Jesus was born (Matthew 1:18-24), baptized (Matthew 3), trained on Earth via the Holy Spirit (Matthew 4, Luke 4), began his Ministry (Matthew 4:12-25, Matthew 5:1-12, Luke 3:23), died on the cross for our sins (Matthew 27) and achieved God's will (Matthew 6:10) for His life – Victory (Matthew 28). Like Jesus, we are all created on purpose for a special purpose (Ephesians 2:10, 1 Peter 2:9-10) to help others find salvation in God (1 Thessalonians 5:9). Help others begin the journey (Matthew 28:18-21) of achieving their own Victory in Christ Jesus (1 Corinthians 15:57).

God's gift to mankind is for all to achieve Victory, so that all may live in sustainable peace (2 Peter 1:1-2), joy on Earth (John 16:24) and eternal life with Him (Romans 6:23). May you and your family live in truth (1 Timothy 2:1-6) and achieve Victory in Christ for generations to come.

God bless you on your journey!

Elizabeth Salamanca-Brosig

M2 = Be Armed in Truth.

I am the Alpha and the Omega, the First and the Last, the Beginning and the End (Revelation 22:13).

In the beginning God created the heavens and the earth (Genesis 1:1).

In the beginning was the Word, and the Word was with God, and the Word was God (John 1:1)

The God who made the world and everything in it is the Lord of heaven and earth and does not live in temples built by human hands. And he is not served by human hands, as if he needed anything. Rather, he himself gives everyone life and breath and everything else. From one man he made all the nations, that they should inhabit the whole earth, and he marked out their appointed times in history and the boundaries of their lands. God did this so that they would seek him and perhaps reach out for him and find him, though he is not far from any one of us. For in him we live and move and have our being. As some of your poets have said, "We are his offspring" (Acts 17:24-28).

So God created mankind in his own image, in the image of God he created them; male and female he created them (Genesis 1:27).

Then the Lord God formed a man from the dust of the ground and breathed into his nostrils the breath of life, and the man became a living being (Genesis 2:7).

But for Adam no suitable helper was found. So the Lord God caused the man to fall into a deep sleep; and while he was sleeping, he took one of the man's rib and then closed up the place with flesh. Then the Lord God made a woman from the rib he had taken out of the man, and he brought her to the man. The man said, "This is now bones of my bones and flesh of my flesh; she shall be called 'woman' for she was taken out of man." That is why a man leaves his father and mother and is united to his wife, and they become one flesh (Genesis 2:20-24).

God blessed them and said to them, "Be fruitful and increase in number; fill the earth and subdue it. Rule over the fish in the sea and the birds in the sky and over every living creature that moves on the ground" (Genesis 1:28).

Children are a heritage from the Lord, offspring a reward from him (Psalm 127:3).

For God did not appoint us to suffer wrath but to receive salvation through our Lord Jesus Christ (1 Thessalonians 5:9).

You, my brothers and sisters, were called to be free. But do not use your freedom to indulge in the flesh; rather, serve one another humbly in love. For the entire law is fulfilled in following this command: " Love your neighbor as yourself " (Galatians 5:13-14).

For God so loved the world that he gave his one and only son (Jesus), that whoever believes in him shall not perish but have eternal life. For God did not send his son into the world to condemn the world, but to save the world through him. Whoever believes in him is not condemned already because whoever does not believe stands condemned already because they have not believed in the name of God's one and only son. This is the verdict: light has come into the world, but people loved darkness instead of light because their deeds were evil. Everyone who does evil hates the light, and will not come into the light for fear that their deeds will be exposed. But whoever lives by the truth comes into the light, so that it may be seen plainly that what they have done has been done in the sight of God (John 3:16-21).

The Son is the image of the invisible God, the firstborn over all creation (Colossians 1:15).

Today in the town of David, a Savior (Jesus) has been born to you; he is the Messiah, the Lord (Luke 2:11).

For to us a child is born, to us a son is given, and the government will be on his shoulders. And he will be called Wonderful Counselor, Mighty God, Everlasting Father, Prince of Peace (Isaiah 9:6).

No one has ever seen God, but the one and only Son (Jesus), who is himself God and is in closest relationship with the Father, has made him known (John 1:18).

He died for us so that, whether we are awake or asleep, we may live together with him. Therefore encourage one another and build each other up just as in fact you are doing (1 Thessalonians 5:10-11).

For our struggle is not against flesh and blood, but against the rulers, against the authorities, against the powers of this dark world and against the spiritual forces of evil in the heavenly realms (Ephesians 6:12).

Jesus answered, "I am the way and the truth and the life. No one comes to the father except through me. If you really know me, you will know my father as well. From now on, you do know him and have seen him" (John 14:6).

For Christ (Jesus) also suffered once for sins, the righteous for the unrighteous, to bring you to God. He was put to death in the body but made alive in the spirit (1 Peter 3:18).

When Jesus spoke again to the people, he said "I am the light of the world. Whoever follows me will never walk in darkness, but will have the light of life" (John 8:12).

Jesus said to her, "I am the resurrection and the life. The one who believes in me will live, even though they die; and whoever lives by believing in me will never die. Do you believe this?" (John 11:25-26).

If you declare with your mouth, "Jesus is Lord, "and believe in your heart that God raised him from the dead, you will be saved. For it is with your heart that you believe and are justified, and it is with your mouth that you profess your faith and are saved. As Scripture says, "Anyone who believes in him will never be put to shame." For there is no difference between Jew and Gentile – the same Lord is Lord for all and richly blesses all who call on him, for, "Everyone who calls on the name of the Lord will be saved" (Romans 10:9-13).

See, I will create new heavens and a new earth. The former things will not be remembered, nor will they come to mind. But be glad and rejoice forever in what I will create… (Isaiah 65:17-18).

Therefore I tell you, do not worry about your life, what you will eat or drink, or about your body, what you will wear. Is not life more than food, and the body more than clothes? Look at the birds of the air; they do not sow or reap or store away in barns, and yet your heavenly Father feeds them. Are you not much more valuable than they? Can any one of you by worrying add a single hour to your life?

And why do you worry about clothes? See how the flowers of the field grow. They do not labor or spin. Yet I tell you that not even Solomon in all of his splendor was dressed like one of these. If that is how God clothes the grass of the field, which is here today and tomorrow is thrown into the fire, will he not much more clothe you - you of little faith? So do not worry, saying 'What shall we eat?' or 'What shall we drink?' or 'What shall we wear?' for the Pagans, run after all these things, and your heavenly father knows that you need them. But seek first the kingdom of God and his righteousness, and all these things will be given to you as well. Therefore do not worry about tomorrow, for tomorrow will worry about itself. Each day has enough trouble of its own (Matthew 6:25-34).

"Forget the former things; do not dwell on the past. See, I am doing a new thing! Now it springs up; do you not perceive it?" I am making a way in the wilderness and streams in the wasteland (Isaiah 43:18-19).

Do not love the world or anything in the world. If anyone loves the world, love for the father is not in them. For everything in the world – the lust of the flesh, the lust of the eyes, and the pride of life – comes not from the father but from the world. The world and its desires pass away. But whoever does the will of God lives forever (1 John 2:15-17).

Do not be carried away by all kinds of strange teachings. It is good for our hearts to be strengthened by grace… (Hebrews 13:9).

Set your minds on things that are above, not on earthly things (Colossians 3:2).

In their hearts, humans plan their course, but the Lord establishes their steps (Proverbs 16:9).

In my distress I called to the Lord; I cried to my God for help. From his temple he heard my voice; my cry came before him; into his ears (Psalm 18:6).

I love the Lord, for he heard my voice, he heard my cry for mercy (Psalm 116:1)

He reached down from on high and took hold of me; he drew me out of deep waters. He rescued me from my powerful enemy. From my foes, who were too strong for me. They confronted me in the day of my disaster, but the Lord was my support. He brought me out into a spacious place; he rescued me because he delighted in me. The Lord has dealt with me according to my righteousness; according to the cleanness of my hands he has rewarded me. For I have kept the ways of the Lord; I am not guilty of turning from my God (Psalm 18:16-21).

The righteousness cry out, and the Lord hears them; he delivers them from all their troubles. The Lord is close to the brokenhearted and saves those who are crushed in spirit. The righteousness person may have many troubles, but the Lord delivers him from them all;…(Psalm 34:17-19).

Therefore, I urge you, brothers and sisters, in view of God's mercy, to offer your bodies as a living sacrifice, holy and pleasing to God – this is your true and proper worship. Do not conform to the pattern of this world, but be transformed by the renewing of your mind. Then you will be able to test and approve what God's will is - his good, pleasing and perfect will (Romans 12:1-2).

It is God's will that you be sanctified: that you should avoid sexual immorality; that each of you should learn to control your own body in a way that is holy and honorable, not in passionate lust like the pagans, who do not know God; and that in this matter no one should wrong or take advantage of a brother or sister. The Lord will punish all those commit such sins, as we told you and warned you before. For God did not call us to be impure, but to live a holy life. Therefore, anyone who rejects this instruction does not reject a human being but God, the very God who gives you his Holy Spirit (1 Thessalonians 4:3-8).

The acts of the flesh are obvious: sexual immorality, impurity and debauchery; idolatry and witchcraft; hatred, discord, jealously, fits of rage, selfish ambition, dissensions, factions and envy; drunkenness, orgies, and the like. I warn you, as I did before, that those who live like this will not inherit the kingdom of God (Galatians 5:19-21).

The Lord makes firm the steps of the one who delights in him; though he may stumble, he will not fall, for the Lord upholds him with his hands (Psalm 37:23-24).

Do not fret because of those who are evil or be envious of those who do wrong; for like the grass they will soon wither, like green plants they will soon die away. Trust in the Lord and do good; dwell in the land and enjoy safe pasture. Take delight in the Lord, and he will give you the desires of your heart. Commit your way to the Lord; trust in him and he will do this: he will make your righteous reward shine like the dawn, your vindication like the noonday sun. Be still before the Lord and wait patiently for him; do not fret when people succeed in their wicked ways, when they carry out their wicked schemes. Refrain from anger and turn from wrath; do not fret – it leads to evil. For those who are evil will be destroyed, but those who hope in the Lord will inherit the land (Psalm 37:1-9).

Jesus replied, "Very truly I tell you, no one can see the kingdom of God unless they are born again" (John 3:3).

Therefore, if anyone is in Christ, the new creation has come: the old has gone, the new is here! (2 Corinthians 5:17).

But Jesus called the children to him and said, "Let the little children come to me, and do not hinder them, for the kingdom of God belongs to such as these. Truly I tell you, anyone who will not receive the kingdom of God like a little child will never enter it" (Luke 18:16-17).

Once, on being asked by the Pharisees when the kingdom of God would come, Jesus replied, "The coming of the kingdom of God is not something that can be observed, nor will people say, 'Here it is' or 'there it is' because the kingdom of God is in your midst" (Luke 17:20-21).

Peter replied, "Repent and be baptized every one of you, in the name of Jesus Christ for the forgiveness of your sins. And you will receive the gift of the Holy Spirit. The promise is for you and your children and for all who are far off- for all whom the Lord our God will call". With many other words he warned them; and he pleaded with them. "Save yourselves from this corrupt generation." Those who accepted his message were baptized, and about three thousand were added to their number that day (Acts 2:38-41).

But you will receive power when the Holy Spirit comes on you; and you will be my witnesses in Jerusalem, and in all Judea and Samaria, and to the ends of the earth (Acts 1:8).

…and this water symbolizes baptism that now saves you also – not the removal of dirt from the body but the pledge of a clear conscience toward God. It saves you by the resurrection of Jesus Christ, who has gone to heaven and is at God's right hand – with angels, authorities and powers in submission to him (1 Peter 3:21-22).

Now the Lord is in the Spirit, and where the Spirit of the Lord is, there is freedom (2 Corinthians 3:17).

"If you love me, keep my commandments. And I will ask the Father, and he will give you another advocate to help you and be with you forever – The Spirit of truth. The world cannot accept him, because it neither sees

him nor know him, for he lives with you and will be with you. I will not leave you as orphans; I will come to you. Before long, the world will not see me anymore, but you will see me. Because I live, you also will live. On that day you will realize that I am in my father, and you are in me, and I am in you. Whoever has my commands and keeps them is the one who loves me. The one who loves me will be loved by my Father, and I too will love them and show myself to them" (John 14:15-21).

But the Advocate, the Holy Spirit, whom the Father will send in my name, will teach you all things and will remind you of everything I have said to you. Peace I leave with you; my peace I give you. I do not give to you as the world gives. Do not let your hearts be troubled and do not be afraid (John 14:26-27).

When you lie down, you will not be afraid; when you lie down, your sleep will be sweet. Have no fear of sudden disaster or of the ruin that overtakes the wicked, for the Lord will be at your side and keep your foot from being snared (Proverbs 3:24-26).

I will instruct you and teach you in the way you should go; I will counsel you with my loving eye on you. Do not be like the horse or the mule, which have no understanding but must be controlled by bit and bridle or they will not come to you (Psalm 32:8-9).

Praise be to the God and Father of our Lord Jesus Christ! In his great mercy he has given us new birth into a living hope through the resurrection of Jesus Christ from the dead, and into an inheritance that can never perish, spoil or fade. This inheritance is kept in heaven for you, who through faith are shielded by God's power until the coming of the salvation that is ready to be revealed in the last time (1 Peter 1: 3-5).

For it is by grace you have been saved, through faith – and this is not from yourselves. It is the gift of God - not by works, so that no one can boast (Ephesians 2:8).

…he saved us, not because of righteous things we have done, but his mercy. He saved us through the washing of rebirth and renewal by the Holy Spirit, whom he poured out on us generously through Jesus Christ our Savior, so that, having been justified by his grace, we might become heirs having the hope of eternal life (Titus 3:5-8).

Therefore, since we have been justified through faith, we have peace with God through our Lord Jesus Christ, through whom we have gained access by faith into this grace in which we now stand (Romans 5:1).

The fear (respect) of the Lord leads to life; then one rests content, untouched by trouble (Proverbs 19:23).

Jesus Christ is the same yesterday and today and forever (Hebrews 13:8).

For those who find me find life and receive favor from the Lord (Proverbs 8:35).

For the wages of sin is death, but the gift of God is eternal life in Christ Jesus our Lord (Romans 6:23).

Jesus said, "My kingdom is not of this world. If it were, my servants would fight to prevent my arrest by the Jewish leaders. But now my kingdom is from another place" (John 18:36).

The thief (The enemy) comes only to steal and kill and destroy; I have come that they may have life, and have it to the full (John 10:10).

Your Dreams Matter.

For you created my inmost being; you knit me together in my mother's womb. I praise you because I am fearfully and wonderfully made; your works are wonderful, I know that full well (Psalm 139:13-14).

Commit to the Lord whatever you do, and he will establish your plans (Proverbs 16:3).

…and to make it your ambition to lead a quiet life: You should mind your own business and work with your hands, just as we told you, so that your daily life may win the respect of outsiders and so that you will not be dependent on anybody (1 Thessalonians 4:11-12).

For I know the plans I have for you," declares the Lord, "plans to prosper you and not to harm you, plans to give you hope and a future (Jeremiah 29:11).

Many are the plans in a person's heart, but it is the Lord's purpose that prevails (Proverbs 19:21).

For the Lord God is a sun and shield; the Lord bestows favor and honor; no good thing does he withhold from those whose walk is blameless. Lord Almighty, blessed is the one who trusts in you (Psalm 84:11-12).

Now to him who is able to do immeasurable more than all we ask or imagine, according to his power that is at work within us, to him be glory in the church and in Christ Jesus throughout all generations, for ever and ever! Amen (Ephesians 3:20).

Like an athlete trains, so
must the student of life.

Similarly, anyone who competes as an athlete does not receive the victor's crown except by competing according to rules (2 Timothy 2:5).

Therefore, since we are surrounded by such a great cloud of witnesses, let us throw off everything that hinders and the sin that so easily entangles. And let us run with perseverance the race marked out for us, fixing our eyes on Jesus, the pioneer and perfecter of faith. For the joy set before him he endured the cross, scorning its shame, and sat down at the right hand of the throne of God. Consider him who endured such opposition from sinners, so that you will not grow weary and lose heart (Hebrews 12:1-3).

For the eyes of the Lord range throughout the earth to strengthen those whose hearts are fully committed to him (2 Chronicles 16:9).

And have you completely forgotten this word of encouragement that addresses you as a father addresses his son? It says, "My son, do not make light of the Lord's discipline, and do not lose heart when he rebukes you, because the Lord disciplines the one he loves, and he chastens everyone he accepts as his son." Endure hardship as discipline; God is treating you as his children, for what children are not disciplined by their father? If you are not disciplined – and everyone undergoes discipline – then you are not legitimate, not true sons and daughters at all. Moreover, we have all had human fathers who disciplined us and we respected them for it. How much more should we submit to the Father of Spirits and live! They disciplined us for a little while as they thought best; but God disciplines us for our good, in order that we may share in his holiness. No discipline seems pleasant at the time, but painful. Later on, however, it produces a harvest of righteousness and peace for those who have trained by it. Therefore, strengthen your feeble arms and weak knees. Make level paths for your feet, so that the lame may not be disabled, but rather healed (Hebrews 12:5-13).

Have nothing to do with godless myths and old wives' tales; rather train yourself to be godly. For physical training is of some value, but godliness has value for all things, holding promise for both the present life and the life to come (1 Timothy 4:7-8).

Train the mind, body and spirit, so you may achieve anything.

The fear (respect) of the Lord is the beginning of knowledge, but fool's despise wisdom and instruction (Proverbs 1:7).

For God is not a God of disorder but of peace- as in all the congregations of the Lord's people (1 Corinthians 14:33).

All Scripture is God-breathed and is useful for teaching, rebuking, correcting and training in righteousness, so that the servant of God may be thoroughly equipped for every good work (2 Timothy 3:16).

Start children off the way they should go, and even when they are old they will not turn from it (Proverbs 22:6).

Love the Lord your God with all your heart and with all your soul and with all your strength. These commandments that I give you today are to be on your hearts. Impress them on your children. Talk about them when you sit at home and when you walk along the road, when you lie down and when you get up. Tie them as symbols on your hands and bind them on your foreheads. Write them on the doorframes of your houses and on your gates (Deuteronomy 6:5-9).

Submit yourselves then, to God. Resist the devil, and he will flee from you. Come near to God and he will come near to you. Wash your hands, you sinners, and purify your hearts, you double-minded (James 4:7-8).

Now the one who has fashioned us for this very purpose is God, who has given us the Spirit as a deposit, guaranteeing what is to come. Therefore we are always confident and know that as long as we are at home in the body we are away from the Lord. For we live by faith, not by sight (2 Corinthians 5:5-7).

Now faith is confidence (Faith in Action) in what we hope for and assurance about what we do not see (Hebrews 11:1).

But what does it say? "The word is near you; it is in your mouth and in your heart, that is, the message of concerning faith that we proclaim: If you declare with your mouth, "Jesus is Lord, "and believe in your heart that God raised him from the dead, you will be saved. For it is with your heart that you believe and are justified, and it is with your mouth that you profess your faith and are saved. As Scripture says, "Anyone who believes in him will never be put to shame." For there is no difference between Jew and Gentile – the same Lord is Lord for all and richly blesses all who call on him, for, "everyone who calls on the name of the Lord will be saved (Romans 10:8-13).

Peter replied, "Repent and be baptized every one of you, in the name of Jesus Christ for the forgiveness of your sins. And you will receive the gift of the Holy Spirit. The promise is for you and your children and for all who are far off- for all whom the Lord our God will call". With many other words he warned them; and he pleaded with them. "Save yourselves from this corrupt generation." Those who accepted his message were baptized, and about three thousand were added to their number that day (Acts 2:38-41).

Do not merely listen to the word, and so deceive yourselves. Do what it says (James 1:22).

"…But as for me and my household, we will serve the Lord" (Joshua 24:15).

"If the world hates you, keep in mind that it hated me first. If you belonged to the world, it would love you as its own. As it is, you do not belong to the world, but I have chosen you out of the world. That is why the world hates you. Remember what I told you: 'A servant is not greater than his master. If they persecuted me, they will persecute you also. If they obeyed my teaching, they will obey yours also. They will treat you this way because of my name, for they do not know the one who sent me. If I had not come and spoken to them, they would not be guilty of sin; but now they have no excuse for their sin. Whoever hates me hates my Father as well. If I had not done among them the works no one else did, they would not be guilty of sin. As it is, they have seen, and yet they have hated both me and my Father. But this is to fulfill what is written in their Law: "They hated me without reason" (John 15:18-25).

The words of the wise are like goads, their collected sayings like firmly embedded nails – given by one shepherd. Be warned, my son of anything in addition to them, of making many books there is no end, and much study wearies the body. Now all has been heard, here is the conclusion of the matter: fear (respect) God and keep his commandments, for this is the duty of all mankind. For God will bring every deed into judgement, including every hidden thing, whether it is good or evil (Ecclesiastes 12:11-14).

The tongue has the power of life and death, and those who love it will eat its fruit (Proverbs 18:21).

And God spoke all these words (The Ten Commandments): I am the Lord your God, who brought you out of Egypt, out of the land of slavery. You shall have no other Gods before me. You shall not make for yourself an image in the form of anything in heaven above or on the Earth beneath or in the waters below. You shall not bow down to them or worship them; for I, the Lord your God, am a jealous God, punishing the children for the sin of the parents to the third and fourth generation of those who hate me, but showing love to a thousand generations of those who love me and keep my commandments. You shall not misuse the name of the Lord your God, for the Lord will not hold anyone guiltless who misuses his name. Remember the Sabbath Day keeping it holy. Six days you shall labor and all your work, but the seventh day is a Sabbath Day to the Lord your God. On it you shall not do any work, neither you, nor your son or daughters, nor your male or female servants, nor your animals, nor any foreigner residing in your towns. For in six days the Lord made the heavens and the Earth, the sea, and all that is in them, but he rested on the seventh day. Therefore the Lord blessed the Sabbath Day and made it holy. Honor your father and mother, so that you may live long in the land the Lord your God is giving you. You shall not murder. You shall not commit adultery. You shall not steal. You shall not give false testimony against your neighbor. You shall not covet your neighbor's house. You shall not covet your neighbor's wife, or his male or female servant, his ox, or donkey, or anything that belongs to your neighbor (Exodus 20:1-17).

Jesus replied: " 'Love the Lord your God with all your heart and with all our soul and with all your mind.' This is the first and greatest commandment. And the second is like it: 'Love your neighbor as yourself.' All the Law and the Prophets hang on these two commandments. (Matthew 22:37-40).

Love your Lord your God with all your heart and with all your soul and with all your mind and with all your strength. The second is this: 'Love your neighbor as yourself.' There is no greater commandment than these (Mark 12:30-31).

A new command I give you: Love one another. As I have loved you, so you must love one another. By this everyone will know that you are my disciples, if you love one another (John 13:34-35).

Love must be sincere. Hate what is evil; cling to what is good. Be devoted to one another in love. Honor one another above yourselves. Never be lacking in zeal, but keep your spiritual fervor, serving the Lord. Be joyful in hope, patient in affliction, faithful in prayer. Share with the Lord's people who are in need. Practice hospitality. Bless those who persecute you; bless and do not curse. Rejoice with those who rejoice; mourn with those who mourn. Live in harmony with one another. Do not be proud, but be willing to associate with people of low position. Do not be conceited. Do not repay anyone evil for evil. Be careful to do what is right in the eyes of everyone. If it is possible, as far as it depends on you, live at peace with everyone. Do not take revenge, my dear friends, but leave room for God's wrath, for it is written: "It is mine to avenge; I will repay," says the Lord. On the contrary: if your enemy is hungry, feed him; If he is thirsty, give him something to drink. In doing this, you will heap burning coals on his head." Do not be overcome by evil, but overcome evil with good (Romans 12:9-21).

For if you forgive other people when they sin against you, your heavenly Father will also forgive you. But if you do not forgive others their sins, your Father will not forgive your sins (Matthew 6:14-15).

I love those who love me, and those who seek me find me (Proverbs 8:17).

Therefore, with minds that are alert and fully sober, set your hope on the grace to be brought to you when Jesus Christ is revealed at his coming. As obedient children, do not conform to the evil desires you had when you lived in ignorance. But just as he who called you is holy, so be holy in all you do; for it is written: "Be holy, because I am holy." Since you call on a Father who judges each person's work impartially, live out your time as foreigners here in reverent fear (respect). For you know that it was not with perishable things such as silver and gold that you were redeemed from the empty way of life handed down to you from your ancestors, but with the precious blood of Christ, a lamb without blemish or defect. He was chosen before the creation of the world, but revealed in these last times for your sake. Through him you believe in God, who raised him from the dead and glorified him, and so your faith and hope are in God. Now that you have purified yourselves by obeying the truth so that you have sincere love for each another, love one another deeply, from the heart. For you have been born again, not of perishable seed, but of imperishable, through the living and enduring word of God. For, "All people are like grass, and all their glory is like the flowers of the field; the grass withers and the flowers fall, but the word of God endures forever." (1 Peter 1:13-25).

The end of all things is near. Therefore be alert and of sober mind so that you may pray. Above all, love each other deeply, because love covers over a multitude of sins. Offer hospitality without grumbling. Each of you should use whatever gift you have received to serve others, as faithful stewards of God's grace in various forms. If anyone speaks, they should do so as one who speaks the very words of God. If anyone serves, they should do so with the strength God provides, so that in all things God may be praised through Jesus Christ. To him be the glory and the power for ever and ever. Amen (1 Peter 4:7-11).

My dear brothers and sisters, take note of this: Everyone should be quick to listen, slow to speak and slow to become angry, because human anger does not produce the righteousness that God desires. Therefore, get rid of all moral filth and the evil that is so prevalent and humbly accept the word planted in you, which can save you. Do not merely listen to the word, and so deceive yourselves. Do what it says (James 1:19-22).

Follow the way of love and eagerly desire the gifts of the Spirit, especially prophecy. For anyone who speaks in a tongue does not speak to people but to God. Indeed, no one understands them; they utter mysteries by the Spirit. But the one who prophesies speaks to people for their strengthening, encouraging and comfort. Anyone who speaks in a tongue edifies themselves, but the one prophesies edifies the church. I would like everyone of you to speak in tongues, but I would rather have you prophesy. The one who prophesies is greater than the one who speaks in tongues, unless someone interprets, so that the church may be edified (1 Corinthians 14:1-5).

Be very careful, then, how you live – not as unwise but as wise, making the most of every opportunity, because the days are evil. Therefore do not be foolish, but understand what the Lord's will is (Ephesians 5:15-17).

For those who are led by the Spirit of God are the children of God. The Spirit you received does not make you slaves, so that you live in fear again; rather, the Spirit you received brought about your adoption in sonship. And by him we cry, "Abba, Father." The Spirit himself testifies with our Spirit that we are God's children. Now if we are children, then we are heirs – heirs of God and co-heirs with Christ, if indeed we share in his sufferings in order that we may also share in his glory (Romans 8:14-17).

But you have an anointing from the Holy Spirit, and all of you know the truth. I do not write to you because you do not know the truth, but because you do know it and because no lie comes from the truth. Who is the liar? It is whoever denies that Jesus is the Christ. Such a person is the antichrist – denying the Father and the Son (1 John 2:20-22).

And this is my prayer: that your love may abound more and more in knowledge and depth of insight, so that you may be able to discern what is best and may be pure and blameless for the day of Christ, filled with the fruit of righteousness that comes through Jesus Christ – to the glory and praise of God (Philippians 1:9-10).

Dear Friends, do not believe every Spirit, but test the Spirits to see whether they are from God, because many false prophets have gone out into the world. This is how you can recognize the Spirit of God: Every Spirit that acknowledges that Jesus Christ has come in the flesh is from God, but every Spirit that does not acknowledge Jesus is not from God. This is the Spirit of the antichrist, which you have heard is coming and even now is already in the world (1 John 4:1-3).

Consider it pure joy, my brothers and sisters whenever you face trials of many kinds, because you know that the testing of your faith produces perseverance. Let perseverance finish its work so that you may be mature and complete, not lacking anything. If any of you lacks wisdom, you should ask God, who gives generously to all without finding fault, and it will be given to you. But when you ask, you must believe and not doubt, because the one who doubts is like a wave of the sea, blown and tossed by the wind. That person should not expect to receive anything from the Lord. Such a person is double-minded and unstable in all they do (James 1:2-7).

Dear friends, do not be surprised at the fiery ordeal that has come on you to test you, as though something strange were happening to you. But rejoice inasmuch as you participate in the sufferings of Christ, so that you may be overjoyed when his glory is revealed. If you are insulted because of the name of Christ, you are blessed. For the Spirit of Glory and of God rests on you. If you suffer, it should not be as a murderer or thief or any other kind of criminal, or even as a meddler. However, if you suffer as a Christian, do not be ashamed, but praise God that you bear that name (1 Peter 4:12-16).

So then, those who suffer according to God's will should commit themselves to their faithful creator and continue to do good (1 Peter 4:19).

Blessed is the one who perseveres under trial because, having stood the test, that person will receive the crown of life that the Lord has promised to those who love him (James 1:12).

But the fruit of the Spirit is love, joy, peace, forbearance, kindness, goodness, faithfulness, gentleness and self-control. Against such things there is no law (Galatians 5:22-23).

In everything set them an example by doing what is good. In your teaching show integrity, seriousness and soundness of speech that cannot be condemned, so that those who oppose you may be ashamed because they have nothing bad to say about us (Titus 2:7-8).

We have different gifts, according to the grace given to each of us. If your gift is prophesying, then prophesy in accordance to your faith, if it is serving, then serve; if it is teaching, then teach; if it is to encourage, then give encouragement; if it is giving, then give generously; if it is to lead, do it diligently; if it is to show mercy, do it cheerfully (Romans 12:6-8).

There are different kinds of gifts, but the same Spirit distributes them. There are different kinds of service, but the same Lord. There are different kinds of working, but in all of them and in everyone it is the same God at work. Now to each one the manifestation of the Spirit is given for the common good. To one there is given through the Spirit a message of wisdom, to another a message of knowledge by means of the same Spirit, to another faith by the same Spirit, to another gifts of healing by that one Spirit, to another miraculous powers, to another prophecy, to another speaking in different kinds of tongues. All these are the work of one and the same Spirit, and he distributes them to each one, just as he determines (1 Corinthians 12:4-11).

Is anyone among you in trouble? Let them pray. Is anyone happy? Let them sing songs of praise. Is anyone among you sick? Let them call the elders of the church to pray over them and anoint them with oil in the name of the Lord. And the prayer offered in faith will make the sick person well; the Lord will raise them up. If they have sinned, they will be forgiven. Therefore confess your sins to each other and pray for each other so that you may be healed. The prayer of a righteous person is powerful and effective (James 5:13-16).

Now we ask you, bothers and sisters, to acknowledge those who work hard among you, who care for you in the Lord and who admonish you, hold them in the highest regard in love because of their work. Live in peace with each other, and we urge you, brothers and sisters, warn those who are idle and disruptive, encourage the disheartened, help the weak, be patient with everyone. Make sure that nobody pays back wrong for wrong, but always strive to do what is good for each other and for everyone else. Rejoice always, pray continually, give thanks in all circumstances; for this is God's will for you in Christ Jesus. Do not quench the Spirit. Do not treat prophecies with contempt but test them all; hold on to what is good, reject every kind of evil. May God himself, the God of peace, sanctify you through and through. May your whole Spirit, soul and body be kept blameless at the coming of the Lord Jesus Christ the one who calls you is faithful, and he will do it. Brothers and sisters, pray for us. Greet all God's people with a holy kiss (1 Thessalonians 5:12-26).

Since, then you have been raised with Christ, set your hearts on things above, where Christ is, seated at the right hand of God. Set your minds on things above, not on Earthly things. For you died, and your life is hidden with Christ in God. When Christ, who is your life appears, then you also will appear with him in glory. Put to death, therefore, whatever belongs to your Earthly nature: sexual immorality, impurity, lust, evil desires and greed, which is idolatry. Because of these, the wrath of God is coming. You used to walk in these ways. In the life you once lived. But now you must also rid yourselves of all such things as these: anger, rage, malice, slander, and filthy language from your lips. Do not lie to each other, since you have taken off your old self with its practices and have put on the new self, which is being renewed in knowledge in the image of its Creator. Here there is no Gentile or Jew, circumcised or uncircumcised, barbarian, Scythian, slave or free, but Christ is all, and is in all. Therefore, as God's chosen people, holy and dearly loved, clothe yourselves with compassion, kindness, humility, gentleness and patience. Bear with each other and forgive one another if any of you has a grievance against someone. Forgive as the Lord forgave you. And over all these virtues put on love, which binds them all together in perfect unity. Let the peace of Christ rule in your hearts, since as members of one body you were called to peace. And be thankful. Let the message of Christ dwell among you richly as you teach and admonish one another with all wisdom through psalms, hymns, and songs from the Spirit, singing to God with gratitude in your hearts. And whatever you do, whether in word or deed, do it all in the name of the Lord Jesus, giving thanks to God the Father through him (Colossians 3:1-17).

Marriage should be honored by all, and the marriage bed kept pure for God will judge the adulterer and all the sexually immoral (Hebrews 13:4).

He who finds a wife finds what is good and receives favor from the Lord (Proverbs 18:22).

To the married I give this command (not I, but the Lord): A wife must not separate from her husband. But if she does, she must remain unmarried or else be reconciled to her husband. And a husband must not divorce his wife (1 Corinthians 7:10-11).

Children are a heritage from the Lord, offspring a reward from him (Psalm 127:3).

Wives, submit yourselves to your husbands, as is fitting in the Lord. Husbands, love your wives and do not be harsh with them. Children, obey your parents in everything, for this pleases the Lord. Fathers, do not embitter your children, or they will become discouraged (Colossians 3:18-21).

She watches over the affairs of her household and does not eat the bread of idleness (Proverbs 31:27).

A woman is bound to her husband as long as he lives. But if her husband dies, she is free to marry anyone she wishes, but he must belong to the Lord (1 Corinthians 7:39).

We hear that some among you are idle and disruptive. They are not busy; they are busybodies. Such people we command and urge in the Lord Jesus Christ to settle down and earn the food they eat. And as for you, brothers and sisters, never tire of doing what is good. Take special note of anyone who does not obey our instruction in this letter. Do not associate with them, in order that they may feel ashamed. Yet do not regard them as enemy, but warn them as you would a fellow believer (2 Thessalonians 3:11-15).

Do not rebuke an older man harshly, but exhort him as if he were your father. Treat younger men as brothers, older women as sisters, with absolute purity. Give proper recognition to those widows who are really in need. But if a widow has children or grandchildren, these should learn first of all to put their religion into practice of caring for their own family and so repaying their parents and grandparents, for this is pleasing to God. The widow who is really in need and left all alone puts her hope in God and continues night and day to pray and to ask God for help. But the widow who lives for pleasure is dead even while she lives. Give the people these instructions, so that no one may be open to blame. Anyone who does not provide for their relatives, and especially for their own household, has denied the faith and is worse than an unbeliever (1 Timothy 5:1-8).

Do not destroy the work of God for the sake of food. All food is clean, but it is wrong for a person to eat anything that causes someone else to stumble (Romans 14:20-21).

Then God said, "I give you every seed-bearing plant on the face of the whole Earth and every tree that has fruit with seed in it. They will be yours for food (Genesis 1:29).

"Please test your servants for ten days: give us nothing but vegetables to eat and water to drink. Then compare our appearance with that of the young men who eat the royal food, and treat your servants in accordance with what you see." So he agreed to this and tested them for ten days. At the end of the ten days they looked healthier and better nourished than any of the young men who ate the royal food (Daniel 1:12-15).

Fruit trees of all kinds will grow on both banks of the river. Their leaves will not wither, nor will their fruit fail. Every month they will bear fruit, because the water from the sanctuary flows to them. Their fruit will serve for food and their leaves for healing (Ezekiel 47:12).

Down the middle of the great street of the city, on each side of the river stood the tree of life, bearing twelve crops of fruit, yielding its fruit every month. And the leaves of the tree are for the healing of the nations (Revelations 22:2).

I ate no choice food; no meat or wine touched my lips; and I used no lotions at all until the three weeks were over (Daniel 10:3).

So that it will not be obvious to others that you are fasting, but only to your Father; who is unseen; and your Father, who sees what is done in secret, will reward you (Matthew 6:18).

Bring the whole tithe into the storehouse, that there may be food in my house. Test me in this, "Says the Lord Almighty," And see if I will not throw open the flood gates of heaven and pour out so much blessing that there will not be room enough to store it (Malachi 3:10).

Keep your lives free from the love of money and be content with what you have, because God has said, "Never will I leave you; never will I forsake you." So we say with confidence, "The Lord is my helper; I will not be afraid. What can mere mortals do to me?" (Hebrews 13:5-6)

No one can serve two masters. Either you will hate the one and love the other, or you will be devoted to the one and despise the other. You cannot serve both God and money (Matthew 6:24).

Then Jesus said to his disciples, "Truly I tell you, it is hard for someone who is rich to enter the kingdom of heaven. Again I tell you, it is easier for a camel to go through the eye of a needle than for someone who is rich to enter the kingdom of God" (Matthew 19:23-24).

In everything I did, I showed you that by this kind of hard work we must help the weak, remembering the words the Lord Jesus himself said: 'It is more blessed to give than to receive" (Acts 20:35).

Give, and it will be given to you. A good measure, pressed down, shaken together and running over, will be poured into you lap. For with the measure you use, it will be measured to you (Luke 6:38).

A cheerful heart is good medicine, but a crushed Spirit dries up the bones (Proverbs 17:22).

In the same way, you who are younger, submit yourselves to your elders, all of you. Clothe yourselves with humility toward one another, because "God opposes the proud but shows favor to the humble." Humble yourselves, therefore, under God's mighty hand, that he may lift you up in due time. Cast all your anxiety on Him because he cares for you. Be alert and of sober mind. Your enemy the devil prowls around like a roaring lion looking for someone to devour. Resist him, standing firm in the faith, because you know that the family of believers throughout the world is undergoing the same kind of sufferings. And the God of all grace, who called you to his eternal glory in Christ, after you have suffered a little while, will himself restore you and make you strong, firm and steadfast. To him be the power for ever and ever Amen (1 Peter 5:5-11).

We who are strong ought to bear with the failings of the weak and not to please ourselves. Each of us should please our neighbors for their good, to build them up (Romans 15:1-2).

Brothers and sisters, if someone is caught in a sin, you who live by the Spirit should restore that person gently. But watch yourselves, or you also may be tempted. Carry each other's burdens, and in this way you will fulfill the Law of Christ (Galatians 6:1-2).

Being confident of this, that he who began a good work in you will carry it on to completion until the day of Christ Jesus (Philippians 1:6).

To the elders among you, I appeal as a fellow elder and a witness of Christ's sufferings who also will share in the glory to be revealed. Be shepherds of God's flock that is under your care, watching over them – not because you must, but because you are willing as God wants you to be; not pursuing dishonest gain, but eager to serve; not lording it over those entrusted to you, but being examples to the flock. And when the Chief Shepherd appears, you will receive the crown of glory that will never fade away. In the same way, you who are younger, submit yourselves to your elders. All of you, clothe yourselves with humility toward one another, because, "God opposes the proud but shows favor to the humble." Humble yourselves, therefore, under God's mighty hand, that he may lift you up in due time (1 Peter 5:1-6).

Cast all your anxiety on him because he cares for you (1 Peter 5:7).

Be alert and of sober mind. Your enemy the devil prowls around like a roaring lion looking for someone to devour. Resist him, standing firm in the faith, because you know that the family of believers throughout the world is undergoing the same kind of sufferings. And the God of all grace, who called you to his eternal glory in Christ, after you have suffered a little while, will himself restore you and make you strong, firm and steadfast. To him be the power for ever and ever. Amen (1 Peter 5:8-11).

Do not judge, or you too will be judged. For in the same way you judge others, you will be judged, and with the measure you use, it will be measured to you (Matthew 7:1-2).

For we must all appear before the judgment seat of Christ, so that each of us may receive what is due us for the things done while in the body, whether good or bad (2 Corinthians 5:10).

And he took bread, gave thanks and broke it, and gave it to them, saying, "This is my body given for you; do this in remembrance of me." In the same way, after the supper he took the cup saying, "This cup is the new covenant in my blood, which is poured out for you." (Luke 22:19-20).

For whenever you eat this bread and drink this cup, you proclaim the Lord's death until he comes (1 Corinthians 11:26).

"I tell you, whoever publicly acknowledges me before others, the Son of Man will also acknowledge before the angels of God (Luke 12:8).

Shout for joy to the Lord, all the earth. Worship the Lord with gladness; come before him with joyful songs. Know that the Lord is God. It is he who made us, and we are his; we are his people, the sheep of his pasture. Enter his gates with thanksgiving and his courts with praise; give thanks to him and praise his name. For the Lord is good and his love endures forever; his faithfulness continues through all generations (Psalm 100).

Come, let us sing for joy to the Lord, let us shout aloud to the Rock of our salvation. Let us come before him with thanksgiving and extol him with music and song. For the Lord is the great God, the great King above all gods. In his hand are the depths of the earth, and the mountain peaks belong to him. The sea is his, for he made it, and his hands formed the dry land. Come, let us bow down in worship, let us kneel before the Lord our Maker; for he is our God and we are the people of his pasture, the flock under his care (Psalm 95:1-7).

Brothers and sisters, we do not want you to be uninformed about those who sleep in death, so that you do not grieve like the rest of mankind, who have no hope. For we believe that Jesus died and rose again, and so we believe that God will bring with Jesus those who have fallen asleep in him. According to the Lord's word, we tell you that we who are still alive, who are left until the coming of the Lord, will certainly not precede those who have fallen asleep. For the Lord himself will come down from heaven, with a loud command, with the voice of the archangel and with the trumpet call of God, and the dead in Christ will rise first. After that, we who are still alive and are left will be caught up together with them in the clouds to meet the Lord in the air. And so we will be with the Lord forever. Therefore encourage one another with these words (1 Thessalonians 4:13-18).

"Do not let your hearts be troubled. You believe in God; believe also in me. My Father's house has many rooms; if that were not so, would I have told you that I am going there to prepare a place for you? And if I go and prepare a place for you, I will come back and take you to be with me that you also may be where I am. You know the way to the place where I am going." (John 14:1-4).

…but those who hope in the Lord will renew their strength. They will soar on wings like eagles; they will run and not grow weary, they will walk and not be faint (Isaiah 40:31).

The light shines in the darkness, and the darkness has not overcome it (John 1:5).

What, then, shall we say in response to these things? If God is for us, who can be against us? (Romans 8:31).

For the Lord your God is the one who goes with you to fight for you against your enemies to give you victory (Deuteronomy 20:4).

Finally, be strong in the Lord and in his mighty power. Put on the full armor of God, so that you can take your stand your stand against the devil's schemes. For our struggle is not against flesh and blood, but against the rulers, against the authorities, against the powers of this dark world and against the spiritual forces of evil in the heavenly realms. Therefore put on the full armor of God, so that when the day of evil comes, you may be able to stand your ground, and after you have done everything, to stand. Stand firm then, with the belt of truth buckled around your waist, with the breastplate of righteousness in place, and with your feet fitted with the readiness that comes from the gospel of peace. In addition to all of this, take up your shield of faith, with which you can extinguish all the flaming arrows of the evil one. Take the helmet of salvation and the sword of the Spirit, which is the word of God. And pray in the Spirit on all occasions with all kinds of prayers and requests. With this in mind, be alert and always keep on praying for all the Lord's people. Pray also for me, that whenever I speak, words may be given me so that I will fearlessly make known the mystery of the gospel, for which I am an ambassador in chains. Pray that I may declare it fearlessly, as I should (Ephesians 6:10-20).

Life is
about sharing
your dreams/purpose
(gifts/passions/talents)
with the world
and helping others
find their way.

For we are called God's handiwork, created in Christ Jesus to do good works, which God prepared in advance for us to do (Ephesians 2:10).

Whatever you do, work at it with all your heart, as working for the Lord, not for human masters, since you know that you will receive an inheritance from the Lord as a reward. It is the Lord Christ you are serving (Colossians 3:23-24).

Each of you should use whatever gift you have received to serve others, as faithful stewards of God's grace in its various forms. If anyone speaks, they should do so as one who speaks the very words of God. If anyone serves, they should do so with the strength God provides, so that in all things God may be praised (1 Peter 4:10-11).

Jesus said, "If you hold on to my teaching, you are really my disciples. Then you will know the truth, and the truth will set you free" (John 8:31-32).

Then Jesus came to them and said, All authority in Heaven and on Earth has been given to me. Therefore go and make disciples of all nations, baptizing them in the name of the Father and of the Son and of the Holy Spirit, and teaching them to obey everything I have commanded you. And surely I am with you always, to the very end of the age (Matthew 28:18-20).

Jesus called his twelve disciples to him and gave him authority to drive out impure spirits and to heal every disease and sickness (Matthew 10:1).

They went out and preached that people should repent. They drove out many demons and anointed many sick people with oil and healed them (Mark 6:12-13).

Dear children, let us not love with words or speech but with actions and in truth (1 John 3:18).

Claim Your Victory!

But thanks be to God! He gives us the victory through our Lord Jesus Christ (1 Corinthians 15:57).

Have mercy on me, O God,
According to your unfailing love;
According to your great compassion
Blot out my transgressions.
Wash away all of my iniquity and cleanse me from my sin.

From I know my transgressions,
And my sin is always before me.
Against you, you only, have I sinned
And done what is evil in your sight;
So you are right in your verdict
And justified when you judge.
Surely, I was sinful at birth.
Sinful from the time my mother conceived me.
Yet you desired faithfulness even in the womb;
You taught me wisdom in that secret place.

Cleanse me with Hyssop, and I will be clean;
Wash me, and I will be clean;
Wash me, and I will be whiter than snow.
Let me hear joy and gladness;
Let the bones you have crushed rejoice.
Hide your face from my sins and blot out all my iniquity.

Create in me a pure heart, O God,
And renew a steadfast Spirit within me.
Do not cast me from your presence or
Take your Holy Spirit from me.
Restore to me the joy of your salvation
And grant me a willing Spirit, to sustain me.

Then I will teach transgressors your ways,
So that sinners will turn back to you.
Deliver me from the guild of bloodshed, O God.
You who are my God my Savior,
And my tongue will sing of your righteousness.

Open my lips, Lord.
And my mouth will declare your praise.
You do not delight in sacrifice, or I would bring it;
You do not pleasure in burnt offerings;
My sacrifice, O God is a broken spirit;
A broken and contrite heart
You, God will not despise.

May it please you to prosper Zion.
To build up the walls of Jerusalem.
Then you will delight in the sacrifices of the righteous.
In burnt offerings offered whole;
Then bulls will be offered on your altar (Psalm 51).

Who has believed our message
and to whom has the arm of the
Lord been revealed?
He grew up before him like a tender shoot,
and like a root out of dry ground.
He had no beauty or majesty to attract us to him,
nothing in his appearance that we
should desire him.
He was despised and rejected by mankind,
a man of suffering, and familiar with pain.
Like one from whom people hide their faces
he was despised, and we held him in low esteem.
Surely he took up our pain
and bore our suffering,
yet we considered him punished by God,
stricken by him, and afflicted.
But he was pierced for our transgressions,
he was crushed for our iniquities;
the punishment that brought us peace was on him,
and by his wounds we are healed.
We all, like sheep, have gone astray,
each of us has turned to our own way;
and the Lord has laid on him
the iniquity of us all.

He was oppressed and afflicted,
yet he did not open his mouth;
he was led like a lamb to the slaughter,
and as a sheep before its shearers is silent,
so he did not open his mouth/
By oppression and judgment he was taken away.
Yet who of his generation protested?
For he was cut off from the land of the living;
for the transgression of my people he was punished.
He was assigned a grave with the wicked,
and with the rich in his death, though he had done no violence,
nor was any deceit in his mouth.

Yet it was the Lord's will to crush him
and cause him to suffer,
and though the Lord make his life
an offering for sin,
he will see his offspring and prolong his days,
and the will of the Lord will prosper
in his hand.
After he has suffered,
he will see the light of life and be
satisfied;
by his knowledge my righteous servant
will justify many,
and he will bear their iniquities.
Therefore I will give him a portion
among the great,
and he will divide the spoils with the
strong,
because he poured out his life unto death,
and was numbered with the transgressors.
For he bore the sin of many,
and made intercession for the transgressors (Isaiah 53).

My son, do not forget my teachings, but keep my commands in your heart, for they will prolong your life many years and bring you peace and prosperity. Let love and faithfulness never leave you; bind them around your neck, write them on the tablet of your heart. Then you win favor and a good name in the sight of God and man. Trust in the Lord with all your heart and lean not on your own understanding; in all your ways submit to him, and he will make your paths straight. Do not be wise in your own eyes; fear (respect) the Lord and shun evil. This will bring health to your body and nourishment to your bones (Proverbs 3:1-8).

The wise inherit honor, but fools get only shame (Proverbs 3:35).

YOUr Dreams MATTER.

Like an athlete trains, so must the student of life.

Train the mind, body and spirit, so you may achieve anything.

Life is about sharing your dreams/purpose (gifts/passions/talents) with the world and helping others find their way.

Begin Your Journey Today.

Obtain a Holy Bible you are most comfortable with and join a Bible-based Church in your community.

May God bless you and your families for generations to come!

cloud9surfing.com

About the Author

ELIZABETH SALAMANCA-BROSIG, PHARMD is an American born, Filipino blooded lover of Jesus, activist, author, and international speaker. Together with the help of her family, she founded Cloud9Surfing Missions which inspires individuals, families and communities with experiences that lead people to victory. She also founded the Surfing His Word Tour and the International Ukulele Ensemble. The Salamanca-Brosig Family make their home in sunny Florida with their children, Kylie and Kai.

Printed in the United States
By Bookmasters